MAMMALS OF DIFFERENT KINDS

MAMMALS OF DIFFERENT KINDS

Phillip and Teresa Coffey

For Mark, James, Christopher and Andrew

ARNOLD - WHEATON

Arnold-Wheaton
A Division of E. J. Arnold & Son Limited
Registered office at
Parkside Lane, Leeds LS11 5TD
and at
Hennock Road, Exeter EX2 8RP

A subsidiary of Pergamon Press Ltd
Headington Hill Hall, Oxford OX3 0BW

Pergamon Press Inc.
Maxwell House, Fairview Park, Elmsford, New York 10523

Pergamon Press Canada Ltd
Suite 104, 150 Consumers Road, Willowdale, Ontario M2J 1P9

Pergamon Press (Australia) Pty Ltd
P.O. Box 544, Potts Point, N.S.W. 2011

Pergamon Press GmbH
Hammerweg 6, D-6242 Kronberg, Federal Republic of Germany

First published 1984

ACKNOWLEDGEMENTS

The authors would like to thank the following individuals and zoos for allowing them to photograph their animals (particular thanks go to the zoo-keepers, who in many cases allowed the authors behind barriers and off view areas to take photographs):

Basle Zoological Gardens (50); Blackpool Zoological Gardens (14, 16); Cotswold Wildlife Park (21, 23, 25, 34); Cricket St Thomas Wildlife Park (22, 27); Frankfurt Zoological Gardens (5, 7, 15, 36, 43); Jersey Wildlife Preservation Trust (2, 6, 10, 12, 46, 49); D. Laffolley (9); Marwell Zoological Society (31, 39); North of England Zoological Society, Chester (4, 17, 18, 32, 38, 44, 45, 48); Scottish National Zoological Park, Edinburgh (47); Whipsnade Zoological Park (37); Wilhelma Zoological and Botanical Gardens, Stuttgart (33); Windsor Safari Park (29); H. Zimmerman (11); Zoological Gardens, Regent's Park (1, 8, 13, 19, 20, 26, 28, 30, 35, 40, 41, 42); Zurich Zoological Gardens, (3, 24).

The authors would also like to thank Jeremy Mallinson and Nick Lindsay for their help with the manuscript.

Printed in Great Britain by A. Wheaton & Co. Ltd, Hennock Road, Exeter

ISBN 0 08-029300-X

INTRODUCTION

We are living in "The Age of Mammals". There are about 4500 species of mammal on earth today. Many live on land; some burrow underground; some swim in rivers or in seas, and others fly in the air.

Before mammals, the reptiles – particularly dinosaurs – dominated the animal kingdom. The Age of Reptiles lasted for 230 million years, and the dinosaurs were still dominant when the first mammals appeared. These early mammals had evolved from mammal-like reptiles. They looked rather like the tree shrews of today. They were not equipped to compete with the large, powerful dinosaurs, and survived this period as tree-living, nocturnal animals.

Then, about 70 million years ago, the dinosaurs became extinct. Scientists do not know for certain why this happened. However, once the dinosaurs had disappeared, mammals quickly took over all the available habitats.

The first and most primitive mammals to evolve were the egg-laying mammals, which are represented in this book by the echidna.

Then came the pouched or marsupial mammals, which include the marsupial mouse and the red kangaroo. Baby marsupials are not very well developed at birth; they continue growing in the mother's pouch, where they are comparatively safe.

Finally, the most successful and advanced mammals to evolve were the placental mammals. Most of the animals in this book belong to this group. The young develop inside the mother, attached to her by a placenta. This is an organ that allows food and oxygen to pass to the embryo and waste material to pass back to the mother.

Fifteen of the nineteen main groups (or orders) of mammals are represented in this book.

There are several characteristics that most mammals have in common:

• Like fishes, amphibians, reptiles and birds, all mammals have a backbone.
• Mammals give birth to live young and feed them on milk at first. Only mammal mothers produce milk in their breasts (the name "mammal" comes from the Latin word *mamma*, which means "breast").
• Mammals spend more time taking care of their young than other animals do.
• Most mammals grow hair. Hair helps keep the body warm, which is important because mammals are warm-blooded (this means that they can produce heat from within their bodies; if they get too hot, they can lose heat by sweating or panting). Because they are warm-blooded, mammals can live in cold climates as well as hot climates.
• Compared to other animals of equal size, mammals usually have large brains. A large brain is thought to indicate higher intelligence.
• Mammals have four types of teeth, used for different purposes: incisors, canines, premolars and molars. Most mammals also have two sets of teeth. The first set, the milk teeth, drops out and is replaced by permanent teeth.

Mammals have all sorts of diets. The aardvark, for example, eats ants, and the white rhino eats grass. Some mammals, such as the puma and the African wild dog, are predators. They feed on other animals.

Animals that might be eaten by others protect themselves in various ways: the porcupine has spines that can be very painful when stuck into a predator's nose; the kudu antelope can defend itself with its large horns; the Grévy zebra's stripes camouflage its body, and the red kangaroo's extremely long back legs help it run away quickly to escape from danger.

A mammal often relies on one of its senses more than the rest. The margay cat, for example, has excellent eyesight, particularly in poor light. The mountain tapir, with its trunk-like nose, has a well-developed sense of smell. The hearing of the pipistrelle bat is so acute that it can find its insect prey at night by echo location. The pygmy hedgehog tenrec's long whiskers are very sensitive to touch; this helps it to find its way in the dark.

At the end of the book you will find charts that give extra information about the characteristics of mammals, suggestions for project work and further reading, and a glossary.

The following mammals appear in this book:

 1. Bruijn's long-nosed echidna
 2. Byrne's marsupial mouse
 3. Matschie's tree kangaroo
 4. red kangaroo
 5. giant anteater
 6. pygmy hedgehog tenrec
 7. North African elephant shrew
 8. tree shrew
 9. pipistrelle
10. ruffed lemur
11. potto
12. silvery marmoset
13. douroucouli
14. De Brazza's monkey
15. hamadryas baboon
16. agile gibbon
17. chimpanzee
18. Arctic fox
19. African wild dog
20. Asiatic black bear
21. red panda
22. racoon
23. short-clawed otter
24. striped hyena
25. puma
26. margay cat
27. Californian sea-lion
28. grey seal
29. Atlantic bottle-nosed dolphin
30. African elephant
31. Grévy's zebra
32. Przewalski's wild horse
33. mountain tapir
34. white rhinoceros
35. aardvark
36. red river hog
37. hippopotamus
38. Arabian camel
39. Formosan sika deer
40. American bison
41. gaur
42. markhor
43. gerenuk
44. greater kudu
45. prairie marmot
46. Sierra Leone striped squirrel
47. Canadian beaver
48. crested porcupine
49. volcano rabbit
50. chinchilla

1 Bruijn's long-nosed echnida

Zaglossus bruijni

Distribution: West New Guinea and Salawati Islands
Habitat: woods and grassland
Diet: termites

Bruijn's (pronounced brine's) long-nosed echidna belongs to a primitive group of mammals that still lay eggs, like their reptile ancestors.

During the breeding season the female develops a fold of skin on her underside. She lays one leathery-shelled egg and pushes it into this pouch. The baby echidna hatches out in the pouch after about ten days, using an egg-tooth to break the shell from the inside, like reptiles do. The baby is very immature, being naked and only twelve millimetres long.

There are two milk glands, but no teats, in the mother's pouch. The milk simply oozes out and the baby laps it up.

When it is six to eight weeks old, the infant is about ten centimetres long and its spines have started to grow. At this stage, the mother leaves the baby in a nest while she searches for food. She uses her strong claws to break open termite mounds, then pushes her long snout into the mound and picks up the termites with her long, sticky tongue. (Instead of teeth, the echidna has a bony ridge inside its mouth which it uses to crush its food.)

Echidnas are not as successful as other mammals at keeping their body temperature even. Depending on the outside temperature, it may fluctuate between 22 °C and 35 °C.

The echidna's body is covered with fur and short, thick quills. If attacked it can quickly dig a hole deep enough to hide its nose and feet, leaving only its spiny back uncovered. It is almost impossible to pick up an echidna in this position.

Echidnas shelter in burrows or rock crevices during the day and come out late in the afternoon and at night.

2 Byrne's marsupial mouse

Dasyuroides byrnei

Distribution: Northern Territory, South Australia and Queensland, Australia
Habitat: desert and semi-desert
Diet: insects, spiders and small animals

Byrne's (pronounced burns) marsupial mouse is larger than its name suggests, being closer to a rat than a mouse in size. Its large eyes and pointed snout certainly give it a mouse-like appearance, but there the similarity ends. Unlike true mice, the marsupial mouse is a carnivore.

The marsupial mouse hunts at night and finds its prey using its senses of sight, smell and hearing. It pounces on animals and kills them with its sharp, pointed teeth.

Marsupial mice spend most of their time on the ground but they can climb quite well. During the day they stay in their burrows, coming out occasionally to bask in the sun. They also seem to enjoy frequent dust- or sand-baths.

The marsupial mouse may use its black, bushy tail to signal to others. The female's pouch is small and noticeable only when she is carrying young.

3   Matschie's tree kangaroo

Dendrolagus matschiei

Distribution: New Guinea
Habitat: dense rain forest
Diet: leaves and fruit

The ancestors of tree kangaroos had short front legs and long back legs for hopping. They were adapted to living on the ground, in open spaces. However, Matschie's (pronounced mashies) tree kangaroo lives in trees, where there are fewer predators and a plentiful supply of food.

Tree kangaroos are agile climbers. Their front and back legs are the same length and they have strong, curved claws and rough skin on the pads of their feet. All this helps them to grip as they climb. They also have a furry tail which helps them to balance.

This species spends most of its time in the trees, but often comes down to feed. It can drop eighteen metres to the ground without injuring itself. On the ground it moves in short hops.

When it rains, the tree kangaroo sits with its head lower than its shoulders, so that the rain can run off its fur. The thick hair on its neck and the back of its head lies "the wrong way", growing towards its nose. The hair on its back grows the usual way, towards the tail.

4 red kangaroo

Macropus rufus

Distribution: widespread throughout Australia
Habitat: grassy plains
Diet: grass and other leaves

Red kangaroos and grey kangaroos are the largest of all the marsupials. Their body length can be as much as 165 centimetres and their tail length up to 107 centimetres.

The red kangaroo lives in a herd, or "mob", of up to a hundred animals that includes males and females of all ages. The males fight amongst themselves to establish which is the strongest. They try to grab their opponent's neck or arms and kick him in the stomach. This can be quite dangerous because they have a huge claw on each foot.

The red kangaroo's long back legs are adapted for fast hopping, and its sturdy tail helps it to balance. When it hops slowly, each leap it takes can measure two metres. At its top speed (58 k.p.h.), each leap may be as much as eight metres long.

The red kangaroo is a plant-eater and "chews the cud". It uses its long, forward-pointing, chisel-shaped incisor teeth to crop grass, which it swallows quickly. Later on it brings the food back up to its mouth from its stomach. Then, with its ridged molars, it grinds the grass into tiny pieces. Bacteria in its stomach and small intestine help to digest the food further. Feeding takes place during the night and early morning.

During the hottest part of the day, the red kangaroo rests, keeping cool by panting and by licking its arms and chest. It is a very hardy animal, and can survive for as long as three months without water.

5 giant anteater

Myrmecophaga tridactyla

Distribution: South and Central America (Costa Rica to northern Argentina)
Habitat: grassland and forest, including swampy areas
Diet: ants and termites

The giant anteater is one of the few mammals that have no teeth. The food it eats does not need to be chewed, so, over the centuries, as it evolved, its jaws have become toothless.

The anteater tears open termite mounds with the large, powerful claws on its front legs. Then it flicks its sticky tongue, which can be up to 60 centimetres long, inside the mound and carries insects, eggs and cocoons into its mouth. Anteaters may eat as many as 30 000 ants and termites in a day. Not surprisingly, they prefer to eat species that do not have large, biting jaws!

The giant anteater walks along on its knuckles, with its claws held out of the way. If attacked, it can rear up on its hind legs and defend itself with its claws. It is also a strong swimmer, which is useful since its grassland habitat is often flooded during the rainy season.

The anteater's hair is quite stiff. On its head the hair is short, but it becomes longer and longer down its back, so that the hair on its tail can be as much as 40 centimetres long. When asleep, the anteater covers its head and body with its long tail.

6 pygmy hedgehog tenrec

Echinops telfairi

Distribution: Madagascar
Habitat: dry, thorny forests and scrubland
Diet: insects and other invertebrates

The hairs on the pygmy hedgehog tenrec's back have evolved to become hard bristles and spines. This helps to protect the tenrec from predators. It can roll up into a ball, like the European hedgehog. Its tail is very short and does not stick out beyond the spines.

The tenrec's eyes are small and it has a poor sense of sight. However, it compensates by having very good senses of smell and hearing. It is thought that it may be able to sense ultrasound and use this to locate its food. The tenrec also has long whiskers near its face that are very sensitive to touch. All these things are very useful, because the tenrec is nocturnal and they help it to find its way about the forest floor at night. The tenrec is also good at climbing.

Its sharp teeth can be used to crush quite hard insects and other invertebrates, such as worms and slugs.

Between April and November in Madagascar, hardly any rain falls and it is also quite cool. During this time, the tenrec becomes inactive and goes into a state of torpor (similar to hibernation). Its body temperature and breathing rate drop, and all its other important bodily functions slow down.

7 North African elephant shrew

Elephantulus rozeti

Distribution: North Africa (Morocco to Libya)
Habitat: desert and rocky areas
Diet: ants, termites and other insects

The North African elephant shrew is a small mammal, weighing only 25 to 50 grams. It looks rather like a jerboa, with a trunk like an elephant's and back legs like those of a kangaroo!

The elephant shrew's long, flexible nose and the hairs growing from the base of the nose are very sensitive to touch. With its nose it sniffs out insects among leaves and loose soil, picking up the noises the insects make with its large ears. The elephant shrew's eyes are also large and they make it look like a mouse.

The elephant shrew has extremely long back legs, so it can hop and jump over long distances. It is active during the day but shelters in rock crevices if it is too hot.

Elephant shrews keep themselves clean by combing the hair on their faces with their front paws.

8 tree shrew

Tupaia glis

Distribution: South-East Asia
Habitat: tropical rain forest
Diet: insects and fruit

For a long time scientists have argued about which group of mammals the tree shrew belongs to. Some said it was a primitive primate, related in some way to lemurs, monkeys and apes. Today most people believe that the tree shrew belongs to the insectivore group of mammals and is most closely related to the elephant shrew.

The tree shrew is a small, squirrel-like mammal that spends nearly all its time in the trees of the tropical rain forest. It has curved claws on all its fingers and toes that help it to grip bark.

A male and female live together in a territory, which they mark with scent. There is an area on the front of the tree shrew's body which produces an oily substance. The shrew mixes this with urine and rubs it on branches to mark its territory. Other tree shrews smell the scent and avoid the area.

At night, the male and female share a nest. When the female is about to have young, the male helps her to line another nest with dried leaves. She gives birth to her young in the new nest, but comes back to the old nest to sleep, returning to her young to suckle and care for them.

9 pipistrelle

Pipistrellus pipistrellus

Distribution: most of Europe, a large part of Asia and North Africa
Habitat: roosting sites such as caves, rock crevices, hollow trees and buildings
Diet: flying insects such as moths, mosquitos and beetles

Bats are the only mammals that can fly by flapping their wings. The wings are made of skin, stretching from the shoulder to the tail and including the fore and hind limbs. The bones of a bat's fingers are extremely long and help to support the wing membrane. The thumb juts out from the wing and acts as a hook, which is useful for climbing on rocks or branches.

The pipistrelle, with a wing-span of nineteen centimetres, is the smallest European bat. It flies at night, with rapid, jerky movements, in search of flying insects. To find them, the bat gives out high-pitched squeaks, then

listens for the echo. It can tell whether the echo comes from a stationary or moving object. (This is known as "echo location".) Human beings cannot hear these sounds. The bat catches insects with its wing or tail membranes, passes them to its mouth and crunches them up with its sharp teeth.

In most areas, insects are not available all year round, so pipistrelles hibernate during the winter, in places such as caves. They huddle together, not so much to keep warm, but to reduce the loss of moisture. Bats cannot survive freezing temperatures.

10 ruffed lemur

Lemur variegatus

Distribution: north-eastern Madagascar
Habitat: forest
Diet: fruit, leaves and flowers

Lemurs are Primates but they are more primitive than monkeys, apes and man. They have a long muzzle, the tip of their nose is moist and they have an acute sense of smell.

Lemurs are adapted to life in the trees. They have good eyesight and their eyes are on the front of the face. They can see things with both eyes, which gives them 3D ("stereoscopic") vision. This helps them to judge distance, something that is very important when the lemurs are jumping from branch to branch. Lemurs' grasping hands and feet give them a sure grip, and their long tail helps them to balance. Ruffed lemurs can actually hang by their back feet to reach food on lower branches.

Ruffed lemurs seem to enjoy sunbathing. They lean back against a branch, with their arms and legs spread out so the sun can warm their bodies.

These are the only large lemurs to build a nest in which the young are born and reared. They live in family groups, and each group defends its territory by making a series of roars that get louder and louder before stopping abruptly.

11 potto

Perodicticus potto

Distribution: Central and West Africa
Habitat: forest
Diet: insects, snails, eggs, small animals, fruit and leaves

During the day, the potto sleeps in the fork of a tree or in a hollow tree. At night, it comes out and searches for food in the forest. Its large, forward-facing eyes are very efficient and the potto is able to see even in very dim light.

The first finger of the potto's hand is much smaller than the rest, and there is a wide gap between the thumb and the other fingers. Its feet are a similar shape to the hands, so the potto can grasp branches in a pincer-like grip with all four limbs. It moves in a slow and deliberate manner, never letting go with one limb unless the other three are firmly holding on. Even so, it can grab insects and small animals quickly with its hands or mouth.

Under the skin at the back of the potto's neck there are some pointed bones that stick out from its spine. No one knows what these are for. They may be sensitive to touch, or they may help protect the potto if it is bitten on the neck by a predator, such as the palm civet.

12 silvery marmoset

Callithrix argentata

Distribution: Brazil
Habitat: tropical rain forest
Diet: sap, bark, leaves, flowers, fruit and insects

Silvery marmosets live in family groups in the forests of the Amazon Basin. They are agile climbers and resemble squirrels when they run along and jump from branch to branch. They cannot grasp with their hands like other monkeys, so the sharp, curved claws at the ends of their fingers help them to grip. The marmoset's tail, which is longer than the rest of its body, helps with balance.

A family group lives in a territory that is marked with scent. The marmosets spread drops of urine over branches, rubbing with their chests.

As they travel about the forest, marmosets communicate with each other using a variety of chirps, trills and whistles. If two neighbouring groups meet, the adult males will try to scare each other off by turning their backs and lifting their tails.

The silvery marmoset's lower front teeth (incisors) are as long as its canines. It uses these teeth together, to gouge out bark on tree trunks. The marmoset laps up the sap that oozes out of the gash in the tree.

13 douroucouli

Aotus trivirgatus

Distribution: South and Central America
Habitat: tropical forest
Diet: fruit, insects and small animals

The douroucouli is sometimes called the night monkey, because it is the only true monkey that is nocturnal. It is also known as the owl monkey, because of its large eyes.

During the daytime, small groups or pairs of douroucoulis sleep in hollow trees, using the same site day after day. At night, they search for food such as fruit, berries, insects, snails, tree frogs and small lizards. They communicate with each other in melodic twitterings and chirpings. The douroucouli has a fold of skin under its chin that can be inflated with air to make its voice deeper and louder. In the early morning, douroucoulis give a loud, howling dawn chorus before settling down to sleep.

They lose little water through sweating because they are inactive during the hottest part of the day. Consequently, they do not have to drink much. Most of the water they need comes from food.

14 De Brazza's monkey

Cercopithecus neglectus

Distribution: Central Africa, including Zaire, Uganda, Cameroun, Central African Republic, Gabon, Kenya and Sudan
Habitat: tropical forests
Diet: wide variety of plant food and insects

De Brazza's monkey is distinguished by its white goatee beard and the patch of orange fur across its forehead. It belongs to a group of tree-living monkeys called "guenons". De Brazza's monkey seems more aloof and sedate than the other guenons, rarely using facial expressions to show its emotions. A group consists of several females and their young, led by an adult male. Other adult males are not tolerated, so when juvenile males mature they must leave the group.

De Brazza's monkeys seem to prefer swampy or riverside forest. If there is any threat of danger, they may leave the trees and escape along the forest floor. They walk with the palms of their hands and the soles of their feet on the ground. They may also swim across streams.

During the day, De Brazza's monkeys constantly roam in search of food. They can quickly stuff food into their cheek pouches and eat it later. Their diet includes fruit, flowers, buds, leaves, tubers and insects.

15 hamadryas baboon

Papio hamadryas

Distribution: Arabia, Egypt, Sudan, Ethiopia and Somalia
Habitat: grassland and rocky hills
Diet: bulbs, tubers, grass, leaves, fruit, eggs and small animals

Hamadryas baboons live in small groups consisting of one mature male and up to nine females with young. Male baboons are bigger and stronger than the females and they are responsible for protecting other group members. Their canine teeth are exceptionally long and can be used as weapons of defence against creatures such as leopards. If a lone male baboon approaches a group, the resident male will warn him off with a "threat yawn", throwing back his head and opening his jaws wide to display his canines. This is usually enough to persuade the intruder to withdraw. Occasionally, fights take place and the winner either retains or takes over leadership of the group.

Hamadryas baboons spend much of the day searching for food, since this is usually scarce. At night, a number of groups gather together to climb up rocks to find safe places to sleep. As many as 750 baboons may share one small area.

16 agile gibbon

Hylobates agilis

Distribution: Malaya and Sumatra
Habitat: forest
Diet: fruit, leaves, buds, flowers, insects, snails, birds' eggs,
nestlings and other small animals

Agile gibbons are related to gorillas, chimpanzees and orang-utans and so belong to the ape family. However, since they are smaller they are known as lesser apes.

Compared to the other apes, agile gibbons are swift and nimble when moving through the trees. They can even catch birds in flight. Their arms, hands and fingers are long and narrow. When they swing under branches from tree to tree, they use their hands as hooks, and with their long arms they can cover distances of up to ten metres. When agile gibbons travel along the ground, they run upright, on their hind legs, with their arms held straight up in the air.

Agile gibbons live in small family groups including a mature male and female who stay together for life. When the offspring mature, they are forced to leave and start up on their own. Each family lives in a territory which they defend by making long-drawn-out howling or whooping noises.

At night, agile gibbons sleep in the trees, but not in nests like other apes. They have hard patches on their rumps that enable them to sit upright on branches for long periods of time. Like other apes, agile gibbons do not have a tail.

17 chimpanzee

Pan troglodytes

Distribution: Equatorial Africa
Habitat: savannah, woodland and rain forest
Diet: leaves, fruit, insects and (occasionally) small animals

Chimpanzees live in social groups of up to a hundred. Social contact is very important, and they spend a lot of time grooming each other. They have a variety of ways of communicating, such as making noises or pulling faces. Male chimps have a very impressive display: their hair stands on end, they stamp the ground, hoot loudly and finally make a two-legged dash through the undergrowth.

The chimpanzee is our closest living relative in the animal kingdom, so we

have more in common with chimpanzees than with any other creature, including the gorilla and orang-utan. Chimpanzees are intelligent. Some have even been taught to use sign language to communicate with people. They are good at solving problems and can make simple tools. For example, a chimpanzee will break off a twig of the correct length and thickness to poke inside a termite mound to "fish" for termites. The insects bite the stick and the chimp pulls out the stick and eats them.

18 Artic fox

Alopex lagopus

Distribution: around the North Pole in Greenland, Canada, northern Scandinavia, U.S.S.R. and Alaska

Habitat: tundra

Diet: small animals, such as lemmings and other rodents, hares, ground-dwelling birds and carrion

Arctic foxes may be either white or blue. A litter of three or four young may include cubs of each colour. White foxes are generally found in areas that have lots of snow for long periods, while blue foxes are more common in areas where there is less snow. The colour of its fur camouflages the Arctic fox so that it blends in with its surroundings. This enables the fox to creep up on its prey without being seen.

In winter, thick hair covers the Arctic fox's feet to keep them warm. When food is scarce, the fox may scavenge meat from animals that have been killed by polar bears.

As the season changes from winter to summer, the colour of the Arctic fox's fur changes. A fox that is white in winter turns brown in summer, whilst a pale-blue fox turns a darker bluish-grey. The thick winter coat falls out in tufts and for a while the fox can look very untidy.

19 African wild dog

Lycaon pictus

Distribution: eastern, central and southern Africa
Habitat: savannah grassland
Diet: gazelles, antelopes, gnus and zebras

African wild dogs usually live in packs of up to 20 individuals but, exceptionally, a pack may number 60.

They spend the hottest part of the day in the shade or in holes in the ground previously dug by hogs or aardvarks. They are active mainly in the morning and late afternoon.

The pack hunts big-game herds, picking on young, injured, sick or weak animals. Pack members may take turns to chase the prey until it is exhausted. Wild dogs can reach speeds of up to 55 k.p.h. and maintain them for some distance. They grab their prey from behind, by the legs or ankles. Then the whole pack pulls the animal down, ripping it to shreds quite quickly. Wild dogs help to keep the populations of gnus, gazelles and antelopes in check. Also, by killing sick animals, they probably stop disease spreading to the healthy ones.

African wild dogs do not bark like domestic dogs, but utter a high-pitched yelp. Like dogs, however, they mark important rocks and posts in their territory with urine.

20 Asiatic black bear

Selenarctos thibetanus

Distribution: southern and South-East Asia.
Habitat: mountain forest up to 4000 metres above sea-level
Diet: acorns, nuts, fruit and animal flesh

This bear has jet-black hair and is distinguished from the American black bear by the cream-coloured "V" on its chest. Because of this marking, it is sometimes known as the moon bear.

Bears are grouped with the meat-eating cats and dogs in the order Carnivora. However, most bears eat mainly plant food. The Asiatic black bear feeds on leaves, berries, fruit, acorns, nuts and some animal flesh. It is a good climber and spends some time in the trees in search of food. If it finds a bees' nest, the bear will not hesitate to take the honey. It may attack and eat other animals, including wild boar and deer, killing its prey with a blow from its massive front legs, which are armed with very strong claws. Generally, the bear avoids man, but will defend itself if attacked.

In some parts of the Asiatic black bear's range, the winters are mild but in areas where the weather is severe, the bear will hibernate.

21 red panda

Ailurus fulgens

Distribution: western China, northern Burma, Sikkim and Nepal
Habitat: mountain bamboo forest up to 4000 metres above sea-level
Diet: fruit, leaves, small mammals and birds

The red panda, along with its larger relative, the giant panda, is thought to be a member of the racoon family. It is sometimes called the lesser panda, and in China is known as the fire fox.

Its thick chestnut-red fur protects it from the cold Himalayan winters. When asleep, the red panda curls up like a cat or dog, with its tail over its shoulder. It washes like a cat, too, licking its paws and rubbing them over its face and ears.

Dawn and dusk are the periods of greatest activity for the red panda, when it searches for food, such as roots, acorns, lichens, bamboo shoots and moss. Occasionally it may eat eggs, nestling birds or mice. Red pandas climb trees with ease, their long, sharp claws helping to grip the bark.

They are solitary animals unless, of course, a female happens to be rearing young. They call other pandas with shrill cries, whistles and birdlike chirping noises and mark out their territory using scent produced at the base of the tail.

22 racoon

Procyon lotor

Distribution: North and Central America
Habitat: forest areas near water
Diet: small animals, roots, shoots and fruit

When racoons were first observed in captivity, they were seen to take their food to water and wash it before eating it. This amused and puzzled the observers. Perhaps racoons were hygenic animals? Or did they wash their food because they liked playing with water? Racoons do not have salivary glands in their mouths, so maybe the water made it easier for them to swallow the food? In fact, the reason is that in the wild racoons search for food in and around water. They are used to feeding on water animals, such as fish, frogs, crayfish, mussels and snails.

Racoons are nocturnal creatures, sleeping during the day in the forks of trees, in hollow trees or in rock crevices. They are expert climbers and also swim well.

The female gives birth in the spring, to as many as seven young, although three or four are the most usual numbers. For the first seven to ten weeks the mother nurses the young in the den; after this they move around with her. When they are a year old they become independent.

In the southern part of their range racoons are active all year round. Further north, where the winters are much colder, they hibernate.

23 short-clawed otter

Amblonyx cinerea

Distribution: South-East Asia, including southern India, southern China, Sumatra, Java,
Borneo and Palawan
Habitat: rivers and swamps
Diet: mussels, snails and crustaceans

Most species of otter have long claws, but, as its name suggests, the short-clawed otter's claws do not stick out beyond the ends of its fingers and toes. The pads on its fingertips are very sensitive, and are used to feel for food in mud or under boulders in the water.

This species of otter lives in groups along river banks or in swampy areas. Like all otters, it is a skilful swimmer. Otters can close their nostrils and ears when underwater. Their ears are small, their body is streamlined and they have short, water-resistant fur, with very soft underfur. They push themselves through the water with their hind feet, which are webbed, and use their powerful tail as a rudder, for steering.

The otter's young, one to four in number, are born in a hole in the river bank, called a "holt". The cubs' eyes open after about 35 days and they can play outside the holt when they are ten to twelve weeks old. Soon after this, the mother teaches them to swim. She may have to push them into the water if they are reluctant to learn!

24 striped hyena

Hyaena hyaena

Distribution: India, western Asia and parts of Africa
Habitat: grassland and scrubland
Diet: animal flesh, including carrion

The striped hyena is a scavenger, which means that it feeds on rotting flesh. To some people, the thought of animals scavenging is repulsive. However, such animals play an important role in nature by keeping the habitat clean and free from disease.

During the day, the striped hyena rests in holes in the ground, or among rocks. In the evening, it emerges to search for food, relying on its sense of smell to find the bodies of dead animals. If challenged, the striped hyena will withdraw, leaving vultures and other meat-eaters to pick the carcass over until only the bones remain. However, the hyena will still get a meal. It has powerful jaws and teeth that can crush even the largest bones of cattle to reach the marrow inside. Hyenas sometimes catch small animals and will also eat fruit and insects.

The striped hyena lives alone or in small family groups. It marks its territory using scent produced in a gland beneath its tail.

Unlike its relative, the spotted hyena, the striped hyena does not laugh.

25 puma

Felis concolor

Distribution: North, Central and South America
Habitat: jungle, grassland, mountains and desert
Diet: mammals up to the size of deer and birds

The puma, sometimes called the mountain lion or cougar, can live in a wider range of habitats than any other species of the cat family. It can survive in the hot, steamy Amazon jungle, the cold slopes of the Andes and Rocky Mountains, or the wilderness areas of the American grasslands. It is an extremely good jumper, and can make leaps of up to twelve metres, even when running uphill.

The puma is generally nocturnal, but will hunt during the day if food is scarce. It eats a wide variety of animals, ranging in size from mice to deer. In some areas, people objected to pumas killing deer because they wanted to shoot the deer themselves. So hunters killed all the pumas. Within a few years, the deer population increased so much that all the available food for the deer was used up. Consequently, thousands of deer starved to death. The pumas had been keeping the deer population stable by killing only the young, weak, sick or injured animals.

26 margay cat

Felis wiedii

Distribution: Mexico to southern Brazil
Habitat: jungle
Diet: small animals, such as rats, squirrels, opossums, monkeys and birds

The margay cat lives among the trees of the tropical rain forests of South and Central America. It jumps and climbs well, and can even climb down a tree trunk head first like a squirrel. It can hang from a branch by one, or two, back feet. When the margay jumps, its long sharp claws spread out to catch hold of the branch. It needs a good sense of balance for these climbing activities!

The margay is nocturnal and, like all cats, has excellent eyesight. Its eyes are large and have a special layer at the back that reflects light, giving improved sight in dim light. The margay's long sensitive whiskers help it to feel things close to its face, tree branches, for example.

Margay cats are generally solitary and do not make a permanent home. The male and female come together to mate, and then separate.

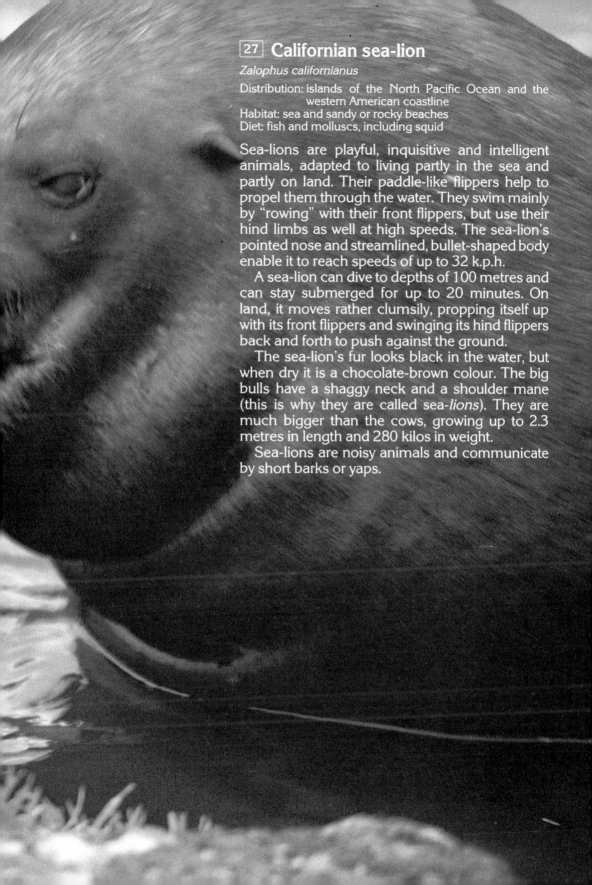

27 | Californian sea-lion

Zalophus californianus

Distribution: islands of the North Pacific Ocean and the
western American coastline
Habitat: sea and sandy or rocky beaches
Diet: fish and molluscs, including squid

Sea-lions are playful, inquisitive and intelligent animals, adapted to living partly in the sea and partly on land. Their paddle-like flippers help to propel them through the water. They swim mainly by "rowing" with their front flippers, but use their hind limbs as well at high speeds. The sea-lion's pointed nose and streamlined, bullet-shaped body enable it to reach speeds of up to 32 k.p.h.

A sea-lion can dive to depths of 100 metres and can stay submerged for up to 20 minutes. On land, it moves rather clumsily, propping itself up with its front flippers and swinging its hind flippers back and forth to push against the ground.

The sea-lion's fur looks black in the water, but when dry it is a chocolate-brown colour. The big bulls have a shaggy neck and a shoulder mane (this is why they are called sea-*lions*). They are much bigger than the cows, growing up to 2.3 metres in length and 280 kilos in weight.

Sea-lions are noisy animals and communicate by short barks or yaps.

28 grey seal

Halichoerus grypus

Distribution: North Atlantic from Labrador eastwards to Novaya Zemlya in the U.S.S.R., and southwards to the Channel Islands and France
Habitat: cool seas
Diet: fish and shellfish, such as prawns, crabs, cockles and whelks

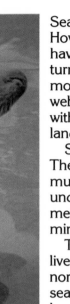

Seals are sometimes confused with sea-lions. However, there are some differences. Seals do not have ear-flaps and their hind limbs cannot be turned forwards like those of sea-lions, so they are more awkward on land. Their back feet are webbed and their forelimbs are short but mobile, with long, curved claws that help them to grip on land.

Seals are well adapted for swimming in the sea. Their bodies are streamlined and they have muscles that close their nostrils while swimming underwater. They can dive down to depths of 128 metres, staying submerged for up to fifteen minutes at a time.

The majority of the world's grey seal population lives in British waters, particularly around the northern rocky shores. During the breeding season, the biggest and strongest bulls collect a harem of six to seven females. The pups are born in October and November. They have a white, woolly, fur coat that they shed four to five weeks later, when the pups are ready to go into the sea.

29 Atlantic bottle-nosed dolphin

Tursiops truncatus

Distribution: Atlantic Ocean
Habitat: warm seas
Diet: fish, squid and shrimps

The Atlantic bottle-nosed dolphin is a toothed whale and belongs to a group of mammals that have returned to living in the sea. It has completely lost its back legs and its front legs have evolved into flippers that are used for steering. The dolphin's body is streamlined and its powerful tail is flattened sideways. The dolphin can reach speeds of 48 k.p.h. and leap three metres clear of the water.

Dolphins have a smooth skin (hair would slow them down in water) and a thick layer of fat, or blubber, which helps to keep them warm. They breathe air through a blow-hole on top of their head. They can make more efficient

use of the available oxygen than land-living mammals, and dive to a depth of 200 metres. Baby dolphins are born tail first, unlike most other mammals. Once the head emerges, the mother pushes the baby to the surface so that it can take its first breath of air.

A dolphin can find food by echo location: it makes a high-pitched noise that bounces off objects, then detects the echo through the bones of its lower jaw. Dolphins communicate with each other by clicks and whistles. They are highly intelligent animals and can be trained to perform tricks and underwater tasks useful to people.

30 African elephant

Loxodonta africana

Distribution: eastern and southern Africa
Habitat: grassland and open forest
Diet: wide range of plant food, including grass, bark, roots and leaves

The African elephant is the largest animal that lives on land: the bulls can grow up to four metres high at the shoulder and weigh as much as six tonnes. Elephants risk becoming over-heated because of their large size, but they lose body heat through their large, fan-like ears.

The elephant's trunk is really an elongated nose and upper lip combined. The trunk is made up of some 40 000 different muscles, so it is very mobile. There are two very sensitive finger-like projections at the tip which the elephant uses to pick up food and examine objects. The elephant uses its trunk to strip leaves and bark from trees, to suck up water and squirt it into its mouth, for breathing and smelling, and for making loud trumpeting noises.

The elephant's tusks are enlarged teeth (upper incisors) and are made of solid ivory. They never stop growing and can be as long as 3.5 metres. Tusks can be used as weapons or to prise bark off trees, and they frequently get broken. The elephant uses its back teeth for chewing. It has a set of four teeth, each of which may be 30 centimetres long. As the teeth are worn down, they are replaced. An elephant has only six sets of teeth, and when the last set wears out it can no longer feed itself and it dies of starvation.

31 Grévy's zebra

Equus grevyi

Distribution: southern Ethiopia, Somalia and northern Kenya
Habitat: savannah and scrub
Diet: grass

Grévy's zebra is the largest of the three main species of zebra (the other two are the plains and the mountain zebra). Grévy's zebra's stripes are narrow and well defined and do not meet under its white belly. It has large, rounded ears and a comparatively short tail. It is a noisy animal. The stallions, in particular, bray loudly like donkeys when they get excited.

The zebra's stripes help to camouflage it amongst grass and shrubs. They break up its outline and make it difficult for predators to see it. Grévy's zebras sometimes band together with oryx and eland to form mixed herds. Larger numbers of animals are more likely to spot predators and raise the alarm. Zebras rely on speed as their main form of defence. Their chief enemy is the lion.

Zebras and horses are so closely related that they can interbreed, although their offspring, called zebroids, cannot reproduce.

32 Przewalski's wild horse

Equus przewalskii

Habitat: grassy plains and desert
Diet: grass and leaves

Przewalski's (pronounced shu-val-ski's) wild horse is the only surviving species of truly wild horse. The others, for example the tarpan, are now extinct. The domestic horse of today is probably descended from two or three species of wild horses that certainly included the tarpan, and possibly Przewalski's wild horse. Other so-called wild horses or "mustangs" are descended from domestic stock that returned to the wild. Przewalski's wild horse, in its purest form, has never been domesticated.

Unlike domestic horses, this species has no forelock, and its dark-brown mane is unusually stiff, almost upright. In the summer its coat is short and smooth, with a thin, dark line along the centre of its back. In the winter its coat grows long and thick to protect it from the biting winds of the open plains.

Przewalski's wild horse lives in small herds of up to twenty animals, led by a single stallion. Other stallions either live alone or band together in bachelor groups.

Once abundant in Central Asia, then limited to the Gobi Desert, this species has not been seen in the wild for some time. Fortunately, however, there is a healthy population of Przewalski's wild horses in zoos and it may become possible to release captive-born animals into their natural habitat.

33 mountain tapir

Tapirus pinchaque

Distribution: Colombia, Ecuador, northern Peru and western Venezuela
Habitat: mountain forests and swamps
Diet: vegetation, such as bark, buds, leaves and fruit

Tapirs are distantly related to the rhinoceros and the horse. All three families have an odd number of toes, with hooves at the end, so they are called odd-toed hoofed mammals.

The mountain or woolly tapir is the smallest of four species of tapir. Its thick coat helps to protect it from the cold weather of the Andes Mountains.

The mountain tapir's snout and upper lip are joined together, forming a small, mobile trunk that it uses to pull food into its mouth. The tapir has a particularly well-developed sense of smell and constantly sniffs the air for signs of danger. It can move its large, trumpet-like ears forwards, backwards or sideways to listen in all directions. Its eyes are small and its eyesight is rather weak.

If the tapir senses danger from a predator, such as a jaguar, it dashes through the dense undergrowth to escape. The skin on the tapir's neck is very tough and is covered with a mane of hair. This helps to protect the tapir's most vulnerable spot (its neck) if it is attacked.

34 white rhinoceros

Ceratotherium simum

Distribution: South Africa, southern Sudan, Zaire and Uganda
Habitat: savannah and brush
Diet: grass

The white rhino is the largest rhinoceros and the second largest land mammal. A full-grown male can weigh over two tonnes and stand two metres high at the shoulders. It is called a *white* rhino because of a misunderstanding of the word *"wijd"* in its Afrikaans name. This word means "wide", and refers to the rhino's lips, not its skin colour, which is in fact grey. The rhino's broad square lips are held close to the ground and are used to crop grass.

The white rhino has little to fear from most predators except, on some

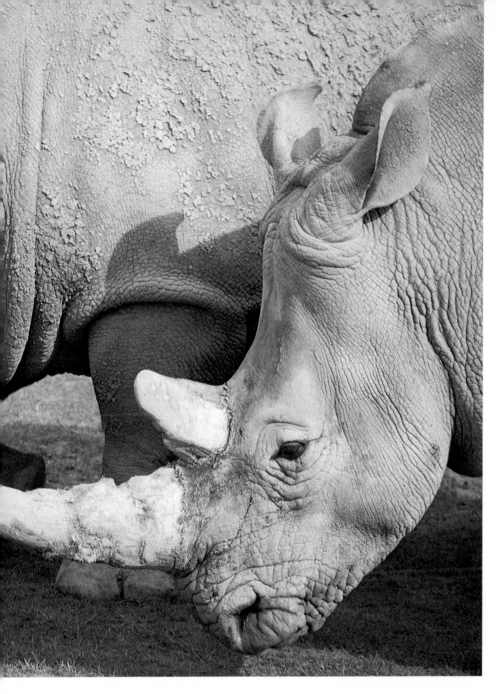

occasions, man. However, it is a cautious animal and remains alert, particularly when a cow is caring for a calf. Rhinos have an acute sense of hearing and smell but their eyesight is poor.

The white rhino frequently associates with tick birds. They eat ticks from its skin and raise the alarm if they see danger.

Rhino horns are made not of bone but of keratin (human hair and fingernails are made of the same material). They grow throughout the rhino's life and if a horn is broken a new one will grow in its place.

35 aardvark

Orycteropus afer

Distribution: Africa, south of the Sahara
Habitat: grassland and open areas
Diet: ants and termites

The name "aardvark" is an Afrikaans word and means "earth-pig". The aardvark has a massive body with a long head and a round, blunt snout with circular nostrils.

The aardvark is very similar in many ways to the South American giant anteater, but they are not closely related. This is a case of two animals adapting in the same way to the same sort of habitat and diet. In fact, the aardvark is not closely related to any other mammal, which is why it is in an order of its own.

A young aardvark develops a full set of teeth, but as it matures the front teeth fall out. An adult needs only back teeth to crush its insect food.

The aardvark breaks open ant nests and termite mounds with its long claws, and uses its long, sticky tongue, which has a coiled tip, to catch the insects. Even if soldier termites swarm over its body, they cannot bite through the aardvark's thick skin.

36 red river hog

Potamochoerus porcus

Distribution: southern Africa
Habitat: forest and thick bush
Diet: roots, bulbs, grass, seeds, fruit, insects, birds' eggs, reptiles and carrion

This hog has distinctive red fur, white and black markings and long tassels of hair on the ears. A member of the pig family, it has a fat, barrel-shaped body, a short neck and a long, pointed head. Its flexible snout has a disc-shaped tip that is quite strong. This is used to dig for food such as roots and bulbs. A herd, or "sounder", of up to twenty of these hogs can cause a lot of damage when feeding in this way, particularly if they happen to be in a farmer's field.

The red river hog's canine teeth, or tusks, can be up to nineteen centimetres long. The shorter, upper tusks wear against the lower ones, helping to keep them sharp. They can be used as weapons when fighting other hogs or in defence against predators. These hogs are courageous fighters and have been known to kill leopards.

They sleep during the day in dense undergrowth, and are active at night.

37 hippopotamus

Hippopotamus amphibius

Distribution: widespread throughout Africa, except desert areas
Habitat: river banks
Diet: grasses and water plants

Hippos are adapted to life on land and in water. Their eyes, ears and nostrils are on top of the head, so they can use their senses when almost submerged. They can remain underwater for up to half an hour, and can walk about on the river bed. When they surface, they can whirl their ears round to clear out the water.

Hippos have no sweat glands. In order to keep cool they spend most of the daytime in the water. If a hippo stays out of water for any length of time, a reddish-brown slime will ooze from the pores in its skin. This slime is thick and oily and it prevents the skin from drying out and cracking. This is what made some people think that hippos "sweat blood".

The hippo's lower canine teeth grow throughout its life and can become enormous. Bull hippos use them as weapons in fights against their rivals.

Hippos come to land at dusk and travel along well-worn paths in search of food. They use their strong lips to crop grass. When they have digested their food they deposit the waste in the water. This feeds microscopic animals that are, in turn, eaten by fishes.

Hippos are distantly related to pigs.

38 Arabian camel

Camelus dromedarius

Distribution: domesticated in North Africa, the Middle East and Asia
Habitat: desert
Diet: desert plants

The Arabian camel was domesticated as early as 4000 B.C. Since then, it has been used as a beast of burden, and as a supplier of milk, meat, skins, wool and fuel (in the form of dried manure). It is sometimes called the dromedary, or one-humped camel.

A camel is ideally suited to life in the desert. It can lose about one quarter of the total amount of water in its body without suffering any ill-effects. Humans would probably die if they lost an eighth. After a period of drought, a camel can drink up to 120 litres of water. This is stored in the stomach and not the hump, which in fact contains fat. When a camel is well fed, the hump stands upright. When food is scarce, the fat is used up and the hump shrinks, sometimes flopping to one side.

A camel is able to feed on plants that other animals reject: its thick lips protect its mouth against spiky desert plants. It has long eyelashes to protect its eyes, and nostrils that can be closed to keep sand out of its nose. The camel's toes (two on each foot) are flattened out to prevent it from sinking into the soft sand.

39 Formosan sika deer

Cervus nippon taiouanus

Distribution: southern Taiwan (formerly Formosa)
Habitat: dense mountain forest
Diet: leaves

The Formosan sika deer is one of thirteen sub-species of sika deer found in South-East Asia. Unfortunately, because of hunting by man and the loss of its habitat, it is on the verge of extinction.

In the summer, the coat of this deer is a rich chestnut-red with many yellowish spots. In the winter it changes to a uniform brown as the spots fade.

Only the males have antlers, which they can use as weapons of defence against predators. The antlers are more often used for fighting other stags at the start of the breeding season (the "rut"). The strongest males usually have the largest antlers, with up to four branches – "tines" – on each. These stags gather the most females. During the rut the stags make a peculiar whistling noise that sometimes changes into a high-pitched scream. When the rut is over the antlers drop off and almost immediately new ones begin to grow.

In the spring each female gives birth to a single calf. The calf is spotted, which camouflages it so that it blends in with the forest floor.

40 American bison

Bison bison

Distribution: once widespread in North America, now found only in wildlife parks
Habitat: prairie grassland
Diet: grass

The bison is the largest land mammal in North America. Adult bulls can weigh almost a tonne, but females weigh only half that amount. The long, thick hair on the bulls' head, neck and shoulders makes them appear even larger.

Once, 60 million bison roamed the prairies, but they were almost wiped out at the end of the last century. They were hunted for meat, hides and sport. The large herds used to migrate hundreds of miles in search of better feeding areas, travelling south to avoid the harsh winters. Several generations of animals would be included in a herd, led by an old cow.

The grass on which bison feed is relatively low in food value, so large quantities are necessary to satisfy their needs. Like deer, cattle, sheep, goats and antelopes, bison chew the cud.

41 gaur

Bos gaurus

Distribution: India, Burma, Malaya
Habitat: deciduous and rain forest
Diet: grass and leaves

The gaur is the largest of all wild cattle. A mature bull may stand 2.2 metres high at the shoulder and weigh about a tonne.

Herds of gaur may number between five and forty animals, led by a master bull. During the heat of the day, they hide in thick forest, coming out to feed in the early morning and evening. They need to drink frequently, and regularly visit water-holes. They have few enemies because of their great size but tigers have been known to kill and eat gaur.

In Malaya this animal is called a *seladang*, and in India it is often referred to as "the Indian bison".

42 markhor

Capra falconeri

Distribution: Himalayas
Habitat: mountain pastures and woods between 1500 and 3600 metres above sea-level
Diet: grass and leaves

The markhor is the world's largest species of goat, standing up to 1.1 metres high at the shoulders. The male has impressive horns shaped like thick corkscrews that may grow up to a metre in length.

High in the Himalayas, the temperature may fall below zero at night, even in the summer. The markhor's thick, shaggy coat protects it against the cold air and the biting winds. Its hair, a rich, reddish-brown in summer, turns grey in winter.

Herds of between five and twenty individuals, led by an adult male, make seasonal migrations. In spring, they move up the mountains to feed above the tree-line, and in winter they move lower down into the forests in the valleys. Markhor are very agile and can climb steep rocky ravines with ease. They can also balance on horizontal branches of the evergreen oak, to browse on its leaves.

The snow leopard is their main predator.

43 gerenuk

Litocranius walleri

Distribution: East Africa (Kenya to Somalia)
Habitat: dry bush country and semi-desert
Diet: leaves

In Somalia, "gerenuk" means "giraffe-necked". This name is very appropriate because the gerenuk has a longer neck than any animal except the giraffe. It can reach leaves on bushes like the acacia by standing on its hind legs, resting its front legs on a tree trunk or even on slender branches for support. The gerenuk has a long muzzle and plucks leaves with its upper lip and tongue. In this way it can obtain food that is out of the reach of many other animals, even larger antelope.

This species can live in semi-desert areas, where shrubs with fresh leaves are scarce. It can also go for long periods without drinking water, surviving on the moisture in the leaves it eats.

Gerenuk live in small herds of up to twelve animals. If there is any threat of danger, they stand absolutely still, and their sandy colouring helps to camouflage them against their surroundings.

Only the males have horns.

44 greater kudu

Tragelaphus strepsiceros

Distribution: widespread throughout Africa in suitable habitat
Habitat: savannah
Diet: leaves on trees and shrubs

The greater kudu is one of the largest antelopes, second only to the eland. An adult male can weigh 270 kilos and stand more than 1.3 metres high at the shoulder.

Only the males have the large spiral horns; these may grow up to 168 centimetres long. They are permanent and are firmly attached to the skull by their bony core. The outer layer is made of keratin, the same material that our nails and hair are made of. Kudu use their horns as weapons, either to defend themselves against predators, or for fighting rival males during the breeding season. For most of the year, adult male kudu live on their own or in small all-male groups.

During the day, kudu hide in secluded areas but come out to feed in the evening and early morning. The white stripes that run down their sides help to break up the outline of their bodies and so camouflage them amongst trees and bushes. They have large ears that they can move in different directions to listen all round. If they sense danger, they run away swiftly. When pursued, they can clear bushes 2.5 metres high with ease.

45 prairie marmot

Cynomys ludovicianus

Distribution: North America
Habitat: prairie grasslands
Diet: leaves and grass

The prairie marmot is well known for the way it lives in large "towns" that may occupy up to 65 hectares of land. These towns have thousands of underground burrows that are linked together, and each burrow has several entrances where the soil is heaped up and then packed down. The piles of earth are thought to prevent heavy rain from flooding the burrows.

Prairie marmots often sit outside their burrows either to feed or bask in the sun. They are constantly alert and if there is any sign of danger, they bark loudly and jump into the air to warn the others. In an instant, all the prairie marmots disappear into their burrows.

The marmot's predators include eagles, rattlesnakes, coyotes, bobcats and people. Once, millions of marmots lived on the open prairies, but many were killed by farmers. The farmers wanted to protect their cattle from stepping into a marmot's burrow and breaking their legs.

Prairie marmots live in small groups that include several females and immature young led by an adult male. Each town is occupied by hundreds of small groups. With mammals, it is usually the young that are forced to find new territory, but in the case of the prairie marmot, the adults migrate, leaving some young in the old burrow.

46 Sierra Leone striped squirrel

Funisciurus pyrrhopus leonis

Distribution: Sierra Leone and Liberia
Habitat: forest, next to clearings
Diet: seeds, nuts, fruit and insects

Sierra Leone striped squirrels are rodents, and belong to a family called the rope squirrels. They live in forests, near clearings where oil palm trees grow. With their sharp claws they can grip bark firmly, so they climb down a tree trunk head first. They come down to the ground to search for food, which is mainly the seeds from the oil palms.

When it is feeding, the squirrel usually holds its long, bushy tail close to its back. If alarmed, the animal will flick its tail smartly and make a loud chucking noise as a warning signal to others.

Sierra Leone striped squirrels normally live in pairs. They build a nest in the fork of a tree, using chewed palm leaves or bark. Usually, two young are born at a time and they share the nest with their parents. These squirrels are active during the daytime. Their eyes are large, and they have good eyesight.

47 Canadian beaver

Castor canadensis

Distribution: North America
Habitat: banks of rivers and lakes
Diet: leaves, bulrushes, tree buds and bark

The Canadian beaver is one of the largest species of rodent, second only to the capybara from South America. It is well known for its ability to gnaw through trees, and can fell a tree eight centimetres thick in about five minutes!

Beavers drag the trees to the water when they have felled them, and use them to build a house or a dam. A beaver will build a dam across a river to create an artificial lake, where it feels secure. The dam may be increased in size up to three metres high and 700 metres long, and with some repair can last for 70 years.

A beaver's home is called a lodge. It is made of sticks cemented together with mud and is strong enough to keep out predators. The foundation of the lodge is on the lake bottom, but its dome-shaped roof is in the air above the surface. There are several entrances to the lodge, at least one of which is underwater. The beaver's sleeping-platform is above the water level inside the lodge.

The beaver is an excellent swimmer, using its webbed feet and broad, flat scaly tail to propel itself through the water. It also uses its tail to smack the surface loudly to warn others of danger.

48 crested porcupine

Hystrix cristata

Distribution: North Africa
Habitat: dry plains and hills
Diet: bulbs, roots, bark, leaves and fruit

The crested porcupine's coat is a mixture of coarse hair and quills. The quills get thicker and longer (up to 40 centimetres long) towards the porcupine's rear. The quills are black, tipped with white, and some of them have tiny barbed hooks.

The porcupine's tail is short, with small, flat quills. These can be shaken together to make a rattling noise that serves as a warning to any would-be predator. The long quills can also be rattled and raised in defence. If it meets an intruder, the porcupine backs towards it. If the animal does not run away, the porcupine will stab it in the nose. This can be quite dangerous, since the quills are difficult to extract and the wound may become infected.

Two or three well-developed young are born at a time and they are able to eat solid food soon after birth. Their quills are short and soft at first.

The porcupine lives on dry plains and hilly slopes. It uses its strong claws to dig burrows where it spends the hottest part of the day.

49 volcano rabbit

Romerolagus diazi

Distribution: Mexico
Habitat: grassy slopes of volcanoes
Diet: young shoots of zacaton grass

Rabbits were once thought to be rodents because their front teeth are chisel-shaped and grow continuously, but there are a number of differences between rabbits and rodents. Rodents have two incisors in the upper jaw, and rabbits have four. Rabbits also have a special way of digesting the tough plant material called cellulose: when the food reaches the part of the gut called the caecum, bacteria begin to digest the cellulose; the food passes out as moist droppings which the rabbit eats, and the goodness is absorbed the second time it passes through the rabbit's body.

The volcano rabbit is different from most other rabbits: it has short ears, dark-brown hair and no tail, and it regularly uses the same paths among the dense tussocks of grass in its habitat. This species is found only on the slopes of the Popocatepetl and Ixtacihuatl volcanoes.

The female gives birth to (usually) two fully furred young, in a burrow.

50 Chinchilla

Chinchilla laniger

Distribution: South America (Peru, Chile and Bolivia)
Habitat: rocky slopes of the Andes
Diet: vegetation

The chinchilla is a rodent and belongs to the same group of mammals as mice, rats, guinea-pigs, squirrels, porcupines and beavers. The chinchilla, like other members of this group, has special front incisor teeth for gnawing. These teeth are very hard on the front edge and soft at the back. As the chinchilla grows, the soft part of the teeth wears down sooner than the hard layer, so that the front edge of each tooth becomes chisel-shaped and very sharp. The incisors keep growing throughout the animal's life.

The chinchilla is most active at night and in the early morning and evening. When feeding it sits on its haunches and holds food in its paws. It does not need to drink water as it gets enough liquid from the plants it eats.

The chinchilla has a thick coat of soft, fine hairs to protect it from the cold weather high up on the mountain slopes. It keeps its fur clean by grooming and by bathing in fine dust. Chinchillas were much sought-after by fur traders and nearly became extinct. Fortunately, however, some traders managed to breed large numbers of chinchillas and this saved the species.

The General Characteristics of Mammals

1. Mammals have a backbone made of smaller bones called vertebrae. (Fish, amphibians, reptiles and birds also have a backbone.)
2. With the exception of the Monotremes, development of the young starts inside the mother's body.
3. The mammal's young are born alive and are fed on milk from the mother's breast.
4. Mammal parents usually take great care of their young.
5. Mammals are warm-blooded.
6. In most cases, a covering of hair insulates the mammal's body and helps with temperature control.
7. The heart has four chambers, which provides a more efficient way of supplying oxygen to the body.
8. There is a thick layer of muscle, called a diaphragm, which separates the lungs from the abdomen.
9. Mammals have four types of teeth, used for different functions: incisors (for picking up food), canines (for stabbing and tearing), pre-molars and molars (for chewing or grinding).
10. Most mammals have two sets of teeth. The first, the milk teeth, is replaced later by a permanent set.
11. There is only one bone in the lower jaw. This particular feature is used by scientists to decide whether fossils are those of reptiles or early mammals.
12. Compared to other animals of equal size, mammals usually have large brains. The area of the brain dealing with intelligence is much more highly developed than in other animals.
13. Mammals have three bones in the middle ear that give them good hearing.
14. Mammals have a bony roof to the mouth (the palate) that separates the mouth from the nose. This means that mammals can chew food and breathe at the same time.

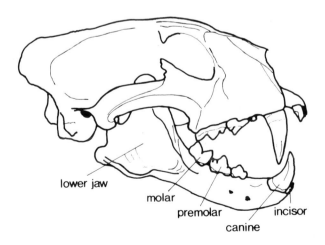

Skull of a leopard, showing the different types of teeth

Main Characteristics of the Different Orders of Mammals

	Order	Examples	Characteristics
1.	Monotremes	spiny anteater, duck-billed platypus	They reproduce by laying eggs. The young are fed on milk but the milk glands do not have teats.
2.	Marsupials	opossums, Byrne's marsupial mouse, red kangaroo, wallaby, koala bear, wombat	The young are born at an immature stage and are reared in a pouch that is supported by special bones. Marsupials have only one set of teeth in their life.
3.	Insectivores	hedgehog, mole, shrew, tree shrew, elephant shrew, pygmy hedgehog tenrec	They usually have a long snout and sharp, pointed teeth for crushing insects.
4.	Flying lemurs*	flying lemur	These mammals have a membrane of skin extending down each side from the neck to the tail. This can be stretched out by the limbs and used for gliding (not flying).
5.	Bats	pipistrelle, horseshoe bat, vampire bat, fruit bat	Flying mammals with wings made of skin.
6.	Primates	ruffed lemur, potto, silvery marmoset, douroucouli, baboon, gibbon, chimpanzee, man	Primates generally live in trees. They have grasping hands and feet, usually with nails instead of claws. They have good eyesight, with stereoscopic vision. The brain is comparatively large.
7.	Edentates	giant anteater, sloth, armadillo	The name "Edentate" means toothless. The anteater is toothless but the sloth and armadillo have molar teeth.
8.	Pangolins*	pangolin (scaly anteater)	The body is covered with overlapping scales that are, in fact, modified hair.
9.	Lagomorphs	hares and rabbits	These mammals have teeth similar to rodents' teeth, but they have an extra pair of incisors in the upper jaw. They eat their droppings, so food passes through the body twice.
10.	Rodents	beaver, squirrel, chinchilla, prairie dog, mouse, rat, guinea-pig, porcupine, capybara	Rodents are gnawing mammals that have four chisel-shaped incisors, two in the top and two in the lower jaw. They do not have canine teeth.

	Order	Examples	Characteristics
11.	Whales	dolphin, porpoise, killer whale, blue whale	Whales are mammals that are adapted to life in water. Their front legs have become flippers, their hind limbs have been lost, and the tail is flattened horizontally for swimming.
12.	Carnivores	civet, mongoose, hyena, cat, cheetah, weasel, badger, otter, dog, fox, racoon, panda, bear	Meat-eating mammals that hunt and kill other animals, carnivores have powerful jaws with large canines for killing and tearing meat, and strong molars for cutting flesh.
13.	Seals	sea-lion, seal, elephant seal	Carnivorous mammals that are adapted to life in the sea. They have four limbs and can move about on land.
14.	Aardvark	aardvark	There is only one species in this group. The only teeth it has are molars, and these are different in structure from those of other mammals.
15.	Elephants	Indian and African elephant	The upper incisors have become tusks and the molar teeth are replaced as they wear out. The nose and upper lip have become elongated to form the trunk.
16.	Hyraxes*	hyrax	The toes have flattened hoof-like nails. Hyraxes are distantly related to elephants.
17.	Sea cows*	dugong, manatee	Plant-eating mammals that are adapted to life in water.
18.	Odd-toed hoofed mammals	tapir, rhinoceros, zebra, ass, horse	These plant-eating mammals usually have an odd number of toes that end in hooves. The body-weight is carried mainly by the middle digit of each foot.
19.	Even-toed hoofed mammals	pig, hippopotamus, camel, giraffe, deer, cattle, sheep, goat, antelope	These plant-eating mammals have an even number of toes that end in hooves. The body-weight is carried equally by the third and fourth toes of each foot.

Not represented in this book.

In some instances, animals that are grouped in a particular order may not have the main characteristics of that order. They are placed there because they have additional features in common with some members of the group; for example, the panda is not a meat-eater but it has a number of characteristics in common with the racoon, so they are both classified as carnivores.

Things to do

If you want to find out more about mammals, there are a number of things you could consider:

• If you live near a zoo, you could study the mammals on display. You could photograph or sketch them and make notes. Try to classify the animals from your own observations, and read the information labels on the enclosures to find out more about those particular animals. Do they have camouflage? Do they use weapons for defence or attack?

• Some museums have collections of stuffed mammals that include large numbers of different species. They may be crowded together in the cases, so you can easily see the differences between closely related mammals. A more modern approach is to show them in a mock-up of their natural habitat. In this way you can see how mammals relate to each other and to creatures such as birds and reptiles. If the museum has a set of mammal skulls on display, you could compare the teeth of rodents, meat-eaters and plant-eaters, etc.

• Quite a few species of mammals have been domesticated and can be found on farms. Some, like the horse, are used as beasts of burden; cows and goats provide milk; cattle, sheep, pigs, rabbits and deer provide meat.

• Many of the more popular pets are mammals, for example rats, mice, gerbils, guinea-pigs, rabbits, cats, dogs and horses. If you have a mammal as a pet, you could study its behaviour. You could try to discover from books how your pet came to be domesticated. Find out about its wild ancestors. How long has the species been domesticated? Which people were responsible?

• If you do not have a pet but are thinking about getting one, then it is important to find out as much as you can beforehand. You have to be sure that you can satisfy the animal's needs. Remember, a pet such as a cat or dog can live for fifteen or more years.

• One mammal that we did not mention earlier in the book is the human species, or *Homo sapiens*. Yes, we are mammals. We are Primates and are most closely related to the apes (the chimpanzee, gorilla and orang-utan). What features do we have that are common to mammals? What do we have in common with the apes? How are we different?

• You could collect pictures of mammals from magazines. When you have enough, group them in different ways, for example: Primates/non-Primates; social/solitary animals; domesticated/wild animals; meat-eaters/plant-eaters; nocturnal/diurnal; land/sea mammals; animals with/without horns.

• Mammals are not easy to study in the wild. British mammals are very interesting but many are nocturnal and so not easily seen. It is more likely that you will see evidence of mammals, for example: molehills, hoof- or footprints, tracks, hair on barbed wire, droppings, rabbit holes, badger sets, partly chewed food showing tooth-marks (squirrels frequently leave the centre part of pine-cones), and bones, including skulls, of dead animals.

Books to read

Animal Life Encyclopaedia (vols 10–13), Bernhard Grzimek. Van Nostrand Reinhold.
Australian Mammals, African Mammals, John Leigh-Pemberton. Animals of the World series, Ladybird.
A Colour Guide to Familiar Animals, Vladimir Hanak. Octopus.
Field Guide to the Mammals of Britain and Europe, F. H. Van Den Brink. Collins.
Guide to Animal Tracks and Signs, Bang and Dahlstrom. Collins.
Handbook of British Mammals, G. B. Corbet and H. N. Southern. Blackwell Scientific Publications.
The Life of Animals with Hooves/Meat Eaters/Monkeys and Apes. Introduction to Nature series, Macdonald Educational.
The Mammals, Richard Carrington. Young Readers' Library, Time-Life International.
Mammals of the World, Mary Parker Buckles. Bantam Books.
The Observer's Book of Wild Animals of the British Isles, Maurice Burton. Warne.
Tracks and Signs, Gwen Allen and Joan Denslow. Clue Books, Oxford University Press.
The World of Mammals, Augusto Vigna Taglianti. Sampson Low.

Glossary

adapt change to be better suited.
bacterium (plural **bacteria**) one of the smallest forms of life. Bacteria can be seen only through a microscope.
browse to feed on twigs and leaves of bushes and shrubs.
camouflaged disguised by colouring or pattern in order to blend in with the background.
carnivore a meat-eater.
carrion dead, rotting animal flesh.
cud food that an animal, such as a cow, brings back into its mouth from its first stomach and chews. The second time the food is swallowed it goes into a different stomach chamber.
dental pad the thick, hard layer cattle have instead of upper incisors. Cattle trap food against the dental pad with their spade-shaped lower incisors and tear it up.
digit finger or toe.
diurnal active during the day (opposite of nocturnal).
domesticated tame, or under human control.
echo location finding things by sending out sounds and listening to the echo.

gland part of the body that makes and releases a substance. For example, a mammary gland produces milk, a sweat gland sweat, and a scent gland scent.

hibernate to spend the winter in an inactive state.

marsupial a mammal that rears its young in a pouch.

membrane a covering or layer, like skin.

muzzle part of an animal's head that includes the nose and mouth.

nestling a bird that is too young to leave the nest.

nocturnal active during the night (opposite of diurnal).

predator an animal that hunts, kills and feeds on other animals.

Primates the name given to the group of mammals that includes lemurs, monkeys, apes and man.

savannah a grassy plain with few trees, in tropical and subtropical regions.

scrub an area of stunted trees and low bushes.

stereoscopic vision the ability to see the same thing with both eyes, giving an impression of depth.

teat a mammal's nipple, which the young sucks to obtain milk.

termite a tropical insect that lives in huge colonies and feeds on wood.

torpid inactive or sluggish.

tree-line line above which trees cannot grow.

ultrasound sound pitched too high for humans to hear.

warm-blooded animal for example a bird or a mammal, whose blood stays at a constant temperature. This is achieved by using food to create heat (heat is released when the food is digested) and by sweating to cool the body when necessary.